MACDONALD STARTERS

Fire

Macdonald Educational

About Macdonald Starters

Macdonald Starters are vocabulary controlled information books for young children. More than ninety per cent of the words in the text will be in the reading vocabulary of the vast majority of young readers. Word and sentence length have also been carefully controlled.

Key new words associated with the topic of each book are repeated with picture explanations in the Starters dictionary at the end. The dictionary can also be used as an index for teaching children to look things up.

Teachers and experts have been consulted on the content and accuracy of the books.

Illustrated by: Michael Ricketts

Editors: Peter Usborne, Su Swallow

Reading consultant: Donald Moyle, author of *The Teaching of Reading* and senior lecturer in education at Edge Hill College of Education

Chairman, teacher advisory panel: F. F. Blackwell, general inspector for schools, London Borough of Croydon, with responsibility for primary education

Teacher panel: Elizabeth Wray, Loveday Harmer, Lynda Snowdon, Joy West

© Macdonald and Company
(Publishers) Limited 1971
Second impression 1971

Made and printed in Great Britain
by Purnell & Sons Limited
Paulton, nr Bristol

First published 1971 by
Macdonald and Company
(Publishers) Limited
St Giles House
49-50 Poland Street
London W1

It's cold.
Daddy makes a fire
with wood and paper.

Daddy lights the paper with a match.
The wood and paper burn.

2

Fire needs air.
The wind blows air on the fire.
The fire burns quickly.

3

The fire is hot.
I must not touch the fire.
4

Daddy puts soil on the fire.
The fire has no air.
The fire goes out.

Sometimes Daddy makes a camp fire.
The camp fire keeps us warm.
Mummy cooks on the camp fire.

Red Indians made fires.
The fires made a lot of smoke.
The Red Indians sent smoke signals.

Houses have chimneys.
The smoke from the fire
goes up the chimney.
8

Cavemen did not have matches.
They rubbed two dry sticks together
to make a fire.

9

The flats are on fire.
The people walk down the fire escape.
The firemen have come in a fire engine.
10

The firemen put out the fire with water.
The water cools the fire.
It puts the fire out.

This man's clothes are on fire.
His friend puts a blanket over him.
The blanket keeps out the air
so the fire will go out.

12

This ship is on fire.
A fire boat has come to put out the fire.

Long ago there was a big fire in London.
It burned for three days.
14

Dry wood burns easily.
This is a forest fire.

In big forests men watch out for smoke.
They put out the fires quickly.

16

Gas burns.
Burning gas makes the water boil.

17

The sun is made of burning gas.
The sun is a very big fire.
18

Deep inside the earth it is very hot.
Sometimes fire comes out of a volcano.

19

Some things melt when they get hot.
The flame makes the candle melt.
20

Very hot fire melts metal.
This man cuts metal with fire.

See for yourself
Fire uses air as it burns.
Put a jar over a candle.
Soon the air in the jar will be gone.
Then the flame will go out.

22

Starter's **Fire** words

wood
(page 1)

paper
(page 1)

match
(page 2)

Red Indian
(page 7)

smoke
(page 7)

chimney
(page 8)

caveman
(page 9)

fire engine
(page 10)

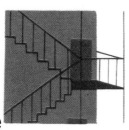

fire escape
(page 10)

fireman
(page 10)

fire boat
(page 13)

forest
(page 15)

gas
(page 17)

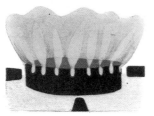

boil
(page 17)

sun
(page 18)

volcano
(page 19)

candle
(page 20)

flame
(page 20)

24